A YEAR TO DISCERN

52 WEEKS OF INTERACTIVE
LEARNING, DISCERNING AND
FINDING YOUR TRUE PURPOSE

BY R. L. MACO

© Copyright 2020 by R. L. Maco

ALL RIGHTS RESERVED. This book contains material protected under International and Federal Copyright Laws and Treaties. Any unauthorized reprint or use of this material is prohibited. No part of this book may be reproduced or transmitted in any form or by any means, electronic or mechanical, including photocopying, recording, or by any information storage and retrieval system, without express written permission from the author/publisher.

ISBN: 978-1-64184-505-2 (hardback)
ISBN: 978-1-64184-506-9 (paperback)
ISBN: 978-1-64184-507-6 (ebook)

INTRODUCTION

Understanding the true meaning and all-encompassing value of *Discernment* is truly a blessing. Once you fully grasp its meaning, utilizing the ability to *Discern* can be scary and calming at the same time. When you are *Discerning*, you often see a different picture than the one presented to you by another, which is a critical part of *Discerning*. *Discerning* means your reasoning skills become sharp or heightened. And although *Discerning* does not mean you will have all the answers to life's questions, the act of *Discerning* allows you to navigate through life on a more conscious level such that it sets the stage for personal growth, development, and accountability. *Discernment* opens the gate for you to enter the realm of enlightenment and empowerment and, if done consistently, sets the environment for you to receive Wisdom. Once you begin *Discerning* regularly, there is no turning back. *Discernment* captures the bigger picture because it overrides one's selfish desires and focuses on thoughtful actions with the ultimate goal of guiding you toward your true purpose in life.

Now before we dive into the process of *Discerning*, it is important to debunk certain myths about *Discernment*. First and foremost, *Discernment* is not an ability that is gifted to some and not others. In my travels, I have discovered that many believe it is a talent or 'Gift' God bestows upon a chosen few. This is not true. More importantly, this belief is detrimental because it carries a subtle negative connotation of God's image. Specifically, it places you in the mindset that God prefers some over others or that God loves some more than others because he gifts the ability to *Discern* only to those he has chosen to revere over the rest of us. Not only is this not true, but if this is your foundational understanding of *Discernment*, then you do not understand *Discernment* at all. If you proceed in life with this mindset, you will neither benefit from the unique power of *Discernment* nor will you absorb the unmatched benefits associated with the ability to *Discern*. Now, while I agree that some of us may be better at *Discerning* than others, *Discerning* is a skill that takes flight when one is intimately acquainted with oneself and God. Our ability to *Discern* will develop and flourish once we refocus our steps with a keen eye towards understanding who we truly are in the eyes of God, where we started, what we are trying to accomplish, and what changes we need to make in our lives in order to proceed on a track of progressive, purposeful and truthful thinking and living. The truth of the matter is, many of us are not *Discerning* because our lives are so cluttered with distractions and force-fed beliefs that we don't take the time to examine why we make the decisions or choices we make or how we end up in the situations we specifically set out to avoid. We find ourselves in unwanted situations and circumstances because of our own actions, not because God wants only certain individuals to *Discern* and others to just fall by the wayside. Rather, we are not *Discerning* because we have not commissioned ourselves to a position of authority in our own lives. In other words, we allow ourselves to be led by just about everything else except the spirit of *Discernment*.

It is critically important for us to understand that the mind is a powerful vessel that will believe whatever we decide or allow to feed it. Therefore, the first lesson in *Discernment* is for you to develop a mindset that is open to receive and accept the source of *Discernment*, the power of *Discernment*, the understanding of *Discernment*, and the implementation of *Discernment* as a life tool. This mindset starts with a positive image of God and an acknowledgment that God is the source of *Discernment*. With this fundamental understanding and mindset towards

BY R. L. MACO | A YEAR TO DISCERN

Discernment, the purpose of this book is to awaken your spirit of *Discernment* and to provide you with the tools necessary to begin the process of *Discerning* on a regular and consistent basis. This book takes you on a yearlong journey of learning how to *Discern* properly and effectively to discover what you were truly placed on this earth to accomplish, according to God's Will. This book will also provide a basis for you to establish order and fulfillment in your life, amongst other things. As you absorb all the knowledge and lessons along the journey, be prepared for a year of enlightenment, wisdom, and pure joy. *Discernment* is the answer you have been searching for no matter what stage of life you are entering, and now is the time to embrace it and allow it to work wonders in your life.

HOW TO USE THIS BOOK

A Year to Discern is the companion book to my book *A Yearn to Discern: Finding Purpose and Fulfillment Through Discernment.* This book invites you on a yearlong journey of developing your ability to *Discern*. The book identifies key core values that you should study, develop, and incorporate into your life as essential tools for what I call "Conscious Living." While this book provides a full calendar year of study, the goal is to use the book to develop a lifelong strategy of strengthening your ability to do the following: (1) *Discern* consistently and properly, (2) handle life's challenges effectively, and (3) keep you on the intended path meant solely for you. In other words, the goal is to keep you, your actions, and your life in alignment with your true purpose in life. This book details a weekly study plan spread out over 52 weeks or one full calendar year. Specifically, the year is broken down into 52 weeks of skill-building as you attain personal growth and development. The 52 weeks are divided into four quarters. Each quarter represents a 13-week plan of core-value and skill building designed to focus on specific areas that will assist you with the following objectives:

1. Heighten your sense of conscious living.

2. Assist you in making necessary changes that will move you forward in life.

3. Build a solid foundation or skill set upon which to increase your ability to *Discern*.

The four quarters of the year are identified by the acronym S.A.L.T: <u>S</u>elf-Analysis, <u>A</u>ction Plan, <u>L</u>ight, and <u>T</u>ransformation.

I. 1st Quarter – Self-Analysis

II. 2nd Quarter – Action Plan

III. 3rd Quarter – Light

IV. 4th Quarter – Transformation

Using the acronym S.A.L.T. to represent this study is no coincidence. An important aspect of fulfilling our purpose in life includes recognizing that we are called upon to be "Salt of the Earth" without ever losing our fervor or "saltiness" for making an impact in the world.[1] The word 'salt' is derived from the Greek words *Hals*, *Hala*, or *Halas*, which means prudence. Concerning our walk with God, it means that as believers in God, we must exercise prudence as we grow in our walk with God. Prudence is not something that should be taken lightly. Prudence means exercising caution, discretion, skill and good judgment in the handling of our affairs. Prudence requires us to position ourselves so that we can learn and grow in order to carry out God's will. In other words, we must work on ourselves first before we can effectively assist others. As we exercise prudence, God will preserve and season us as we continue to grow as believers. We then go out to be salt in the world. This is why the acronym S.A.L.T. is so important because it represents our progression from self-awareness to transformation. It underscores the fact that in order for us to be that 'Salt of the Earth', our lives must be transformed in many ways. We must exercise prudence in preparing ourselves for the ultimate goal of serving others.

Sure, we all get discouraged at different times in life; but discouragement does not mean we give up Hope or stop forging ahead to fulfill our mission. Each one of us is uniquely designed

---

[1] Holy Bible.

to continue being Salt in the world by learning, reflecting, listening, and consistently renewing our minds through knowledge and understanding. As we do this, if we choose to "Live Consciously"—gaining wisdom, stripping away the selfishness, dropping the fear, and taking control of the insecurities that have led us astray time and time again—then by the end of this yearlong study of personal growth, development, and understanding of God's unique purpose for you, you will have all the tools necessary to *Discern* and navigate your way through life and head directly towards your purpose.

However, staying on course to fulfill your purpose requires you to unlearn certain unhealthy habits that you developed during your life. Instead, you must develop new healthy habits that work in your favor. The journey may not be an easy one, and in many respects, it may be humbling. But in the end, you will see within your vision measurable changes, goals, and objectives that were previously elusive to you for so long. This positive transformation will come into sharp focus so long as you stay the course. But keep in mind that the journey does not stop after the 52 weeks of core-value/skill building study is completed.

On the contrary, the journey is just beginning and will continue throughout life. The road to fulfilling your true purpose is a lifelong journey that continues to provide lessons and learning for as long as you are on the earth. Remember, as Salt, we must continue to keep our saltiness and not lose flavor. That means we must be alert, willing to learn, *Discerning*, become stewards of discipline, and, most importantly, maintain an intimate connection with God throughout life. Making this level of commitment in your life makes the impossible possible. This is the mindset we were meant to have. So, let's begin our *52 Weeks of Interactive Learning, Discerning and Finding Your True Purpose.*

I. SELF-ANALYSIS REPROGRAMMING YOUR MIND

Weeks 1–13

Week 1 – Prayer

Prayer opens the heart and mind; it strengthens the unique connection between you and God and opens the door for free flowing of information, honesty and vulnerability that serves to move you closer towards God so that you can understand your true purpose in life according to His Will, not yours.

MINDSET: Prayer opens all doors, channels, and possibilities to all that God has in store for you.

LESSON:

1. Start each day with a prayer.
2. End each day with a prayer.
3. If at any point in the day you are moved to pray, take a moment, and pray.

We must start the foundation of *Discernment* with prayer. Prayer is the single most important element that will develop and heighten your ability to *Discern*. Prayer is a foundational life tool because it places you in the correct mind frame to strengthen your ability to *Discern*. Why is prayer so important? Remember, the ability to *Discern* is a gift from God, a gift that is given to one and all. God is always rooting for us to take in the lessons, hear the message, and take on the mission of true purpose. Unfortunately, many of us fail to heed the signs or decide to get off course by allowing different distractors to pull us away from our intended goal in life. But guess what? Our reset button is in prayer, and it is available to us 24/7. Prayer is available to you at a moment's notice. In other words, you are always connected with God because we are created by God in his image. Therefore, you are always invited by God to deepen that connection. Prayer is the direct line of divine access that each of us has with God that no one else can disconnect. Too many of us do not understand that we have this level of access to God, so we never tap into this power. If we did, we would know just how abundantly we'd live on so many levels. This is why I find it necessary to explain in detail why your ability to *Discern* starts with the power of prayer.

Prayer allows us to practice what I call "Conscious Living," which is when you live your life on a more focused or heightened level by not allowing your life to become a routine or habitual merry-go-round that you can neither explain nor understand. Conscious Living means that we understand ourselves through the eyes of God, and we have spent time making sense of our past and present in order to secure our future. Conscious Living is about self-reflecting and understanding that authentic self that God made and called you to be. It is also about you loving yourself so you can love others and see your existence and role in the world more clearly. This first quarter of study dealing with Self-Analysis is all about Conscious Living, and it begins with prayer.

Prayer keeps us alert, heightens our awareness, and raises our consciousness in our actions, words, and thoughts. I am always amazed at how prayer changes my outlook in the midst of a trying day. However, the key point about prayer is that it deepens the relationship with God such that you can hear the *Discerning* voice of God. That *Discerning* voice keeps you on the road to your true purpose in life. When done consistently, prayer opens the heart and mind so you can receive the *Discerning* voice of God that translates into your ability to *Discern*. This *Discerning* voice of God is unique to each of us and comes from God in various forms. That unique relationship you develop with God through prayer forges the path to the purpose God designed for you at birth. Prayer heals, refocuses, and opens the flood gates to all possibilities, and makes hope tangible. Prayer leads to *Discernment*.

As you continue to pray for understanding and clarity of purpose, one of the most important aspects of prayer is that it helps you distinguish between detours and distractions. Let me explain the difference between the two:

A <u>Detour</u> is a temporary change in course that must be taken due to a minor setback in the road. The purpose of a detour is to provide you with a temporary alternative course that is specifically designed to lead you back to the course you started on, that is, the rightful course you are following to arrive at your proper destination. What is important to understand about a detour is that it is mapped out for you by someone who has knowledge of the original route you are taking. The person who maps out the detour for you designs it so that it places you back on course. If you follow the detour, you will reach your intended destination so long as you follow the detour signs. Now here is the salient point: the person who designed the detour wants you to get back on the right course. In other words, the person has your best interests in mind when creating the alternative course. Many times in our lives, God provides us with a detour. The problem with detours is that we often think we have a better alternative route in mind that can get us back on course faster, so we ignore the detour and forge our own path. This is us trying to take control over the situation without realizing that we're setting ourselves up for failure. By doing this, we actually get lost and get completely off course, or we severely delay our arrival and miss out on important lessons and rewards because we are no longer where we should be. In many instances, we are going around and around in circles, essentially going nowhere. Our need to be in control and our impatience is what leads us astray. We must understand that detours are a part of life and we have to know when we are confronted with a detour so that we do not panic but stay the course in order to arrive safely at our destination.

On the other hand, a <u>Distraction</u> is an alternative course that is not temporary and designed to take you off your rightful course and place you on another path that is not in alignment with your purpose. It's interesting that many times when we're confronted by a distraction, we allow the distraction to take control of our path but yet when a detour is presented to us, we are quick to not accept it and change course. It is imperative that you learn the difference between a detour and a distraction. A major part of the problem is that we allow our circumstances to dictate our actions. Unfortunately, using our circumstances as the catalyst to make decisions almost always gets us into trouble. The lesson here is that we need to learn to exercise restraint when appropriate and allow God to direct our steps and also know when God requires us to move in a new direction. This is where praying comes into play. Praying to God is what allows us to gain the clarity we need in the world to know the difference between a detour and a distraction. Prayer is that tool to get closer to God, understand his Will, obtain clarity, provide focus and position us for a number of benefits that will keep us focused on the Will of God. Working on your prayer life is the first step to changing your life positively in multiple areas.

If you are finding it difficult to start praying regularly or you are having trouble knowing what to pray for, start out praying for the following:

a. Thankfulness
b. Humanity
c. Healing
d. Understanding
e. Compassion for others
f. Wisdom

g. Hope
h. Confidence

It's difficult to pray for others when you have internal issues of selfishness, hurt and pain going on within. As you continue praying, before you know it, you will see the difference in your walk, perspective, relationships, and a host of changes that will enhance your life and those around you. Focus this week on developing your prayer life, but do not stop after the first week. Continue to pray every day and see your life change drastically.

As a starting point in your prayers, in the space below, make a list of all the things in life you are thankful for and begin praying on each of the things you are thankful for at the beginning of each day.

Thankful Prayers

_____
_____
_____
_____
_____
_____
_____
_____
_____
_____
_____
_____
_____

Week 2 – Vulnerability

Being vulnerable before God allows you to be your true authentic self without filters, airs, or false-pretenses. It is how we become honest with ourselves and gives us the ability to be completely authentic exactly the way God intended us to be.

MINDSET: Be honest like you have never been before.

LESSON: During my prayers and quiet time with myself, I will be vulnerable and peel back all the layers and masks I've worn for so long. I will relearn Me!

The reason why we commence the study with prayer is because prayer opens the door for everything else we do. Prayer leads directly to vulnerability. We pray first to get into the right frame of mind to ask and seek guidance from God. We are asking God's assistance in knowing and understanding what we need to do to position ourselves properly so that we may recognize, acknowledge, receive, and fulfill our divine purpose, according to His Will.

Each of us is starting this study at different levels and at different stages of our lives. Some of us are more guarded than others, some are less trusting than others, and some are less forgiving than others. The list goes on and on. That's why we must pray first to ask God to strip away all the layers, barriers, roadblocks, and blinders so we can get to the heart of who we are. This may take some time, but the goal is to be completely vulnerable and honest with God because doing so ignites your journey of understanding of him and understanding of yourself. The truth of the matter is this: God knows you anyway, whether you know it or not; God knows you better than anyone else. What he needs you to do is acknowledge his authority and stop pretending that you know everything. God wants you to be honest with him even though he knows all there is to know about you. He needs you to understand this fact and for you to show your understanding through your actions. You need to lay all of your fears, insecurities, dreams, anger, and everything else in between before God and converse with him during your prayers with complete honesty. There is nothing off the table when you are speaking with God. And if you get into the habit of praying to God honestly, you will see your prayer life develop and you will gain clarity on how and what to pray about at any given time in your life. Your prayer life is your salvation, and it starts the healing process. By healing, I mean it starts the process of healing all the wounds that you allowed to consume, hurt, or keep you stagnant in life. Once you understand that God is in control, the path becomes clearer to you, and you will see yourself for who you are and who you were intended to be. Being vulnerable heals and gets you back to the authenticity of YOU and not who others think you should be. Be vulnerable before God.

In the space below, write down what you need to be most vulnerable about, perhaps something you haven't shared with anyone before because you were afraid of being judged. Now is the time to release these sore wounds and speak to God about them.

What Do I Need to be Most Vulnerable About before God?

_____
_____
_____
_____
_____
_____
_____
_____
_____
_____
_____
_____
_____
_____
_____
_____
_____
_____
_____
_____
_____
_____

Week 3 – Self-Reflection

Self-Reflection is about spending one-on-one time with yourself for the purpose of understanding who you are and the person God intended you to be. Self-Reflection is the best investment you can make in yourself that will lead to rewards designed to make you a better person as you mature in your understanding of self and your understanding of God.

MINDSET: I am open to understanding who I was, who I am now, and who God intended me to be. I will look at understanding my past, present so I can step positively into my future.

LESSON: I will learn to take control over my actions, words, and thoughts. I will learn to also take responsibility and accountability for myself and the energy I place into the universe.

Once vulnerability, complete honesty, and your authentic self are on the table before God, you set the stage for understanding, wisdom, and enlightenment to enter your personal space. You can now begin to self-reflect on the path where you began, the path you are currently on, and the path you were intended to walk. The goal of self-reflection is to gain a keener understanding of who you are, identify your strengths and weaknesses, and to make necessary changes for you to achieve personal development and growth. You are self-reflecting to get back to your uniqueness, so that God can work his magic in you. Remember, God created you to be unlike anyone else. And until you get back to that unique self, you are not able to fulfill your purpose the way God intended. Self-reflection takes you back to that uniqueness, especially when you reflect upon how you were in childhood. Ask yourself, *Where did that carefree, happy person I was back then disappear to? Am I angry today? Why am I so angry? What is causing this anger? What do I have control over to make this anger go away?*

These are just examples of some questions that will come forth as you continue to self-reflect. Get into the habit of self-reflecting as often as possible. Make it a point to self-reflect at least once a week to trace your actions, words, and thoughts. Think about conflicts that arise along the way and how you deal with them. Think about whether you immediately give up when a crisis arises? If you do, ask yourself why?

We self-reflect to understand what we did, what we are doing, and why we continue to do what we do. As we continue to self-reflect, we will discover things about ourselves that we may want to overlook; things that may have caused us and others harm. This is about confronting ourselves and making necessary changes in order to preserve our authentic self and live out our unique purpose. Starting with prayer, vulnerability, and re-establishing that connection with God helps us with self-reflection. Ultimately, it gets us in the mindset of authenticity and preserves our uniqueness. From there, the path to true purpose will follow.

In the space below, make a list of all the unique characteristics/attributes that make up who you are. Start to reflect on your life.

What Are the Unique Characteristics That Make up Who I Am?

Week 4 – Self-Love

Self-Love is about loving yourself, trusting yourself, respecting yourself, and forgiving yourself. It's about laying aside the guilt, anger and hurt that has stumped your personal growth. Self-Love is Self-Care and it starts with how you view yourself.

MINDSET: God made me out of Love. I am Love, and I am worthy of giving and receiving Love.

LESSON: Love conquers all. Once I learn to Love God and myself, I will overflow with Love for others.

Love must start with a love of God and self. Once we realize that God loves us all, and we were made in his image, we realize that we were made in love. More importantly, we were made for love. Love is the greatest of equalizers that soothes the soul. Love heals the broken and wounded and has the unique power to elevate the heart and mind to levels of fulfillment and Conscious Living that are life-altering if you so allow your heart to receive it. There is nothing more glorious to experience in this world than Love. Love is energy, action, and hope, amongst other things. And when you lead with Love in your heart and mind, hope is always beside you during calm seas and particularly during stormy weather. In other words, Love is the key ingredient to a life of fulfillment and purpose, and it must be consistent and completely understood.

Therefore, self-love is not only a must, but it must come first, for if you do not love yourself, you will not love anyone else, even if you try. We work on Love in the fourth week of this study and not week one because we must first prepare our hearts and minds through prayer to receive Love. We must then reflect on the ways in which we have not shown Love to ourselves by way of what we've done and perhaps what we continue to do. We must also release our painful past and learn how to show Love to ourselves by elevating how we think, speak, and act. Get into the habit of telling yourself that you Love yourself. Hug yourself tight, look in the mirror, smile, and say the words "I Love You." Know that you are worthy of Love. You are love! And as you continue through each day, know that Love means taking care of yourself. Some of us feel as if self-care is an act of selfishness. That is not true. In fact, self-care/self-love is not selfish at all. And it is important to know the difference between the two so you can practice self-care as part of your self-improvement, personal growth, and development regimen. Let's briefly discuss the differences between selfishness and self-care.

Selfishness vs. Self-Care

Selfishness is a burden, not a benefit to oneself. It is a way of thinking that focuses solely on oneself to obtain one's desires/wants at the expense of others. Selfishness does not focus on what a person needs, but what a person wants. It is a false belief that one adopts to believe that they are getting ahead in life. However, the truth is that selfish people regress on several fronts. The selfish person fails to understand that we were not placed on this earth to achieve selfish wants as a goal in life. The more the selfish person takes from another, the more he solidifies his future of unhappiness and unfulfillment. He is one who takes two steps forward and ten steps back. A selfish person is a wounded, hurt person who is dangerous. He is dangerous because he is operating in survival mode and will do anything to survive, including hurt you.

A selfish person doesn't understand that selfishness tricks you into thinking that you are getting ahead until it is too late. The selfish person is never happy for a long or consistent period of time; he experiences pockets of contentedness that dissipates quickly. He believes he has to continue the cycle of selfishness by focusing only on what he wants at all costs. He has the mentality of one who feels entitled. And if you are in his way, he will find a way around you or through you if you do not tap into your ability to *Discern* to get out of the way. This selfishness can only be discontinued by adherence to a process of Consciously Living that includes a mind renewal to change the trajectory of one's life. Living a selfish life leads you down a dead-end street.

Self-Care, on the other hand, is not about being selfish. Self-Care is a form of self-love that is performed as an act of love and preservation of oneself in order to be effective in life and for purposes of ensuring that one is operating at an optimal level. There is nothing selfish about that. Self-care is how we reset, clear our minds for the moment, and recharge if we expect to be good to ourselves and others. Self-care is not about selfish desires but knowing when to take a step back and think of the bigger picture. A major part of self-care is the realization that for one to be effective, you must periodically check in with yourself to see what you're doing and how well you are doing it. Selfishness does not do this. Self-care is not just about acts; it is also about thoughts and words. And although self-care is you taking care of yourself, the goal is to focus solely on yourself TEMPORARILY to serve a greater purpose that extends well beyond you. The premise behind self-care is that you cannot effectively take care of others if you do not take care of yourself first. The analogy I use in the book *A Yearn to Discern* is: when you are on an airplane, and there is a loss in cabin pressure, you must put on your oxygen mask first before you can help others. In other words, you cannot effectively help others out of a negative situation if you are operating from a negative disposition.

The lesson here is knowing the difference between selfishness and self-care. Learn to practice self-care as the first step in understanding Love and take it to the next level of loving others. You will be glad you did.

In the space below, make a list of all the things that you love about you. I'm sure there is so much to love about you. Write everything you love about you—and I mean EVERYTHING!

What Do I Love about Myself?

_____
_____
_____
_____
_____
_____
_____
_____
_____

How Do I Practice Self-Care?

_____
_____
_____
_____
_____
_____
_____
_____
_____

Week 5 – Acceptance

Acceptance is about accepting the authentic person that God made you to be, not the person who everyone wants you to be or the person you convinced yourself that you are.

MINDSET: I accept me because I am unique, unlike anyone else that God has created. God made me the way I am for a reason, and I accept and respect all of me.

LESSON: Acceptance is a form of self-love that should be realized.

Now that certain foundational elements have been set in place, it is time for you to accept who you are. Accepting oneself comes as we learn to love ourselves. While we learn more about ourselves, our manners, our characteristics, our complete self, we will uncover things about ourselves that we want to change. We will get to change in a subsequent week, but for now, we must understand who we are. We must understand how we've been functioning and what changes we may need to make. However, we must first accept who we are and who God made us to be.

As you go through this process, week by week, you will realize that changes will need to be made because you may be operating on someone else's agenda and not living the life you were meant to live. If so, you need to get back to that authentic self, that unique person God made you to be for a specific purpose in the world. Do we need to make changes in life? Yes, we do. But those necessary changes can be made once you take the time to know who you really are. You need to accept your authentic self and make changes to get back to that person. When you accept who you are, you can still recognize your shortcomings and work on managing them. For example, if you are naturally a shy person or an introvert, that may have stopped you from speaking up for yourself at times when you felt you should. As you got older, you may have fought this by trying to be more social or by attending events, such as parties, that would make you more outgoing. However, if part of your core self is that shy, quiet type, then that is who you are. But that doesn't mean you cannot learn to be more outgoing as needed for a job or to speak up for your child at school. In other words, it doesn't have to stop you from progressing in life. You will revert to that quiet, shy person because that is who you are. But instead of looking at your introverted nature as something to be eradicated, your goal is to manage it and be more outgoing as warranted by the situation to accomplish specific goals for specific purposes.

As your ability to *Discern* sharpens, you will learn how to do this appropriately. But for now, learn who you are and accept that person. Acceptance follows learning to love yourself and brings you to another level of awareness. We are now starting to liberate ourselves with self-acceptance. What a blessing!

In the space below, write out those aspects of your authentic self, your core self, that you have learned to accept; things that you've struggled with in the past and you now realize makes up the uniqueness of who you are.

Core Characteristics of Who I Am

_____
_____
_____
_____
_____
_____
_____
_____
_____
_____
_____
_____
_____
_____
_____
_____
_____
_____
_____
_____

Week 6 – Humility

Humbling yourself means that you place arrogance and pride aside so that you can move forward in life. It is attaining a level of freedom that flows from acceptance of who you are in relation to God, not Man.

MINDSET: Pride and arrogance blinds while humility clears. I will lead with humility as a guiding principle in life.

LESSON: I will humble myself in relation to God; I shall not compare myself to Man. I know who I am and who I belong to—knowing that I belong to God is critical.

Knowing the real you can be a humbling experience. Don't be afraid of finally understanding you, but let's be clear by what we mean when we speak of humility. While some definitions of humility include having "a modest or low view of one's own importance,"[2] that is not what we mean when we speak of humility here. In no way should you have a low view of yourself, especially as you continue with this study. On the contrary, when we speak of humility, we are referring to you and your relation to God, the Creator, not Man. This is

---

[2] Oxford Dictionary.

about you recognizing God's authority in your life. God does not mean for you to feel inferior to anyone. However, he does want you to recognize and submit to his authority in your life so that you may tap into your power within that he bestowed upon you. Do you see how this perspective changes everything? Humility also means you free yourself from pride or arrogance, two dispositions that cause numerous problems in life.

Learning to be humble may be a tall order for some, depending upon what you discover about yourself, how you've been operating in life, and for what length of time. But take heart that humility will bring you closer to God and closer to peace and abundance. This is a short lesson that contains so much power as a life lesson. As you continue to pray, incorporate being humble into your prayers and ask God to assist you with being humble. This increases the intimate relationship between you and God, and that's a win-win scenario.

Are you prideful or arrogant? Write down situations in which you allowed your pride or arrogance to dictate the outcome of the situation to your detriment.

Instances Where I Allowed Pride/Arrogance to Get in the Way

___
___
___
___
___
___
___
___
___
___
___
___
___
___
___
___
___
___
___
___
___
___
___
___

Week 7 – Forgiveness

Forgiveness starts with forgiving yourself for being so hard on yourself and not accepting yourself for who you are. Work on forgiving yourself for all the pain and hurt you have been carrying around as baggage. Once you let go of this baggage, then you can focus on forgiveness of others.

MINDSET: I will forgive myself, lay blame at the door, and emerge stronger with an open heart.

LESSON: I will forgive myself for any mistakes I have made along the way. As I forgive myself, I will learn to forgive others whether they accept my forgiveness or not. As I forgive, I will move forward on a clear path to enlightenment.

Many of us have difficulty forgiving others because we feel others may have wronged us, or we allowed pride, anger and arrogance block our willingness to forgive. But how can we even discuss forgiving others when we haven't even forgiven ourselves? As our hearts become more open throughout this study, we become more forgiving. And as you learn more about your authentic self, you will realize you have acted in ways that directly contradict who you really are. For example, you may have felt insecure about your worth and decided not to apply yourself to a job, or perhaps you compared yourself to someone and felt inferior for some reason. Or maybe when you were growing up, you mistreated a sibling because you felt ignored by your parents at the time. There can be hundreds of things you need to forgive yourself for, and it is now time for you to forgive yourself. Once you understand how misguided you were when you did certain things at the time, you will be able to sympathize with others who have made similar mistakes under similar or even different circumstances.

Forgiveness releases you from a stronghold rooted in stubbornness, selfishness, and the need to be "right." But guess what? You are already working on these areas, so you're improving. Forgiveness will set you free. Once you free yourself, you will free others. What a great mental place for you to enter!

In the space provided, write down all the things you've done to yourself that you need to forgive yourself for.

What Do I Need to Forgive Myself For?

_____
_____
_____
_____
_____
_____
_____
_____
_____
_____

Are There People in My Life that I Need to Forgive? Write down who and why you need to forgive them.

_____
_____
_____
_____
_____
_____
_____
_____
_____
_____

Week 8 – Attitude

Your attitude can overshadow talent, true worth and knowledge by dictating an outcome inconsistent with your calling or your authentic self. Develop a positive attitude as a springboard to developing a better and more successful you, in accordance with God's Will.

MINDSET: Attitude can be one of my biggest strengths or greatest weaknesses. I will develop my attitude with purpose and focus.

LESSON: I will take inventory of my attitude and adjust accordingly in relation to my authentic self and God's Will.

You may have heard it before: "Your attitude sucks!" Maybe you heard it said to someone else, or maybe it was said to you. Either way, now is a great time to take inventory of your attitude and how it may have played a role in where you are today: *What type of attitude do I have? Why is my attitude what it is? What is affecting my attitude? Do I display a particular attitude directed at certain people, or do I have the same attitude with everyone I come in contact with? Do people tell me to change my attitude? If so, why? Is my attitude a defense mechanism I use to cover up hurt and pain in my life?* These are just some questions you should ask yourself if your attitude has been a sore spot in your life.

We talked about self-reflection in Week Three and, make no mistake about it, exploring your attitude should be part of your self-reflection process. You want to get to the heart of what is driving your attitude. You should also consider if something happened in your life that caused a shift in your attitude. And again, if your attitude changes depending upon the person you're interacting with, the question you need to ask yourself is why. It all goes back to understanding who you really are, and that continues to happen as each week unfolds. But as the weeks progress, you don't just move on to the next week's study, you bring along what you learned each week and continue to build upon it. Attitude is extremely important because it can negate everything you worked towards. It can also be a front that you present to others because you fail to deal with other areas of your life. Take the time to understand your attitude so you can use it to your advantage. Your attitude shouldn't be a barrier to getting ahead in life, it should be the gateway to opportunities for you.

In the space below, write down ways in which you need to work on your attitude. Are you sarcastic, dismissive of others, etc.?

Qualities That Make up My Attitude

___
___
___
___
___
___
___
___
___
___
___
___
___
___
___
___
___
___
___
___
___
___
___

Week 9 – Meekness

Meekness is a state of mind that allows you to conduct yourself in a disciplined manner where you see beyond your circumstances and focus on longevity, legacy, completeness and purpose.

MINDSET: Meekness is a disposition that comes through analysis of oneself with an understanding of one's goals. Temporary setbacks are just that and will not allow me to stray off course because I am meek, and I am focused on the end goal, not minor distractions.

LESSON: Don't be fooled by another's definition of the word Meek. Meekness is attributed to the strong. Remember, Jesus was Meek. There is strength in being meek because a meek person uses knowledge and obedience to God for strength. The meek do not shrink when waters become rough. Instead, the Meek understands that temporary suffering is a part of life, but that with suffering comes great reward. Meekness is not for the faint at heart. Meekness is for the strong-willed.

Meekness! Now there's a word we don't use very often in our vocabulary. Several definitions are associated with the word Meek, including the quality of being submissive, weak, or acquiescent; essentially, it is viewed as someone who allows themselves to be dominated or controlled. This may be the definition of Meek if your acts and works are focused on pleasing man. But as we continue to study, we learn that we do not belong to man, and what we do going forward is not to please man. On the contrary, our sights are set on pleasing God. Once we understand this critical piece of information, we then realize the power of the Meek and the attributes of the Meek from God's point of view: righteous, teachable, patient, humble, restrained.

Meekness is a controlled strength by those who understand God's role in their life. When you understand who you are and whose you are (meaning you belong to God), then you consider your actions and steps and decide against making quick or premature actions or responses. The Bible tells us that "Blessed are the meek, for they shall inherit the earth."[3] Therefore, the Meek are not intimidated or afraid of their current circumstances because they understand that there is a Horizon, a bigger picture that is the primary focus. The Meek accepts defeat as temporary suffering, learning opportunities, and teachable moments to bring forth a brighter tomorrow. Worrying and complaining are not part of the Meek mindset because the Meek know that everything is ultimately in God's hands. God has the ability to change all situations. Mentally, being Meek is a turning point and the catalyst for greater understanding and further personal development that also heals and replenishes the soul.

---

[3] Matthew 5:5 ESV.

Do you consider yourself to be a meek person? Why or why not? State your reasoning below.

My Attitude Toward Meekness

_____
_____
_____
_____
_____
_____
_____
_____
_____
_____
_____
_____
_____
_____
_____
_____
_____
_____
_____
_____
_____

Week 10 – Delayed Gratification

Delayed Gratification is a concept that is grasped by the Meek and sparks the beginning stages of disciple and a goal-oriented mindset.

MINDSET: I will implement the concept of delayed gratification as a tool of discipline.

LESSON: I will focus on assessing my needs first, not wants. My goal is to set my sights on future, lasting success and happiness that will permeate my life and overflow abundantly for my prosperity and my legacy.

Knowing the value of delayed gratification is one of the biggest overlooked tools used to build wealth and sustain longevity in just about every aspect of your life that you can imagine. Understanding the true definition of the word meek helps understand delayed gratification; that's why meekness is discussed in the previous week. When you understand the bigger picture, you can quell the fears inside and not allow yourself to make rash decisions that will hold you back in the long run. Spending money unnecessarily or responding to others irrationally without a proper analysis leads to regret and unnecessary problems. Learn the value of patience so you can determine when to move now and when to act later. Regret is a painful way to learn a lesson, and that's not what you are trying to accomplish. Stay the course and reap the great rewards of what you sowed.

Do you believe in the concept of delayed gratification? Why or why not? If you do, write down the current ways in which you are delaying gratification because you are more focused on long-term goals.

How I Incorporate Delayed Gratification into My Life

_____
_____
_____
_____
_____
_____
_____
_____
_____
_____
_____
_____
_____
_____
_____
_____
_____
_____

Week 11 – Gratitude

Living in gratitude is to live in complete joy and understanding of the blessings and honor that has been bestowed upon you.

MINDSET: I am grateful because I know how far I've come and where I'm going. Being grateful is a privilege because it comes with a level of understanding that places setbacks, adversity and tragedy into perspective.

LESSON: I am grateful because I am loved, always hopeful, and I know life has more great things in store for me than I can ever imagine.

Being grateful is a wondrous way to navigate through the world because it has a way of humbling you and bringing you back to center when things start to unravel. Gratitude helps you count blessings instead of focusing on tragedies or failures. Do you see how your mind is being renewed? Practice being grateful each day as part of your prayer time to increase your joy meter. Once you realize just how much you have in life, you will be able to handle situations that threaten to steal your joy because you'll realize two things: 1) No one can steal your joy unless you allow someone to, and 2) Gratitude is not something you feel on some days. It is an everyday occurrence that will keep you in good spirits and keep you on task.

What obstacles have you overcome that made you more grateful over the years? Write them down in the space below.

Why I Live in Gratitude

Week 12 – Perception

If you want to change your reality, start with your perception. What you place in your mind will grow like wildfire, so plant wisely.

MINDSET: Perception shapes reality. What I believe, so shall I become. Therefore, I will make sure my perception is shaped by God's point of view.

LESSON: My perception of God, myself, and the world will shape my reality. It is important to know my perceptions in life; my perception has an effect on my view of the world and my place in it.

Now that Week 12 is upon us, you should notice that the seeds you planted over the past 11 weeks have sprouted in the form of awareness. This is an awareness of self, an awareness of others, and an awareness of thoughts, actions, and words. This awareness is only the beginning stages of the 52-Week process, but it is extremely important. The continuation of all the lessons you soaked up over these past weeks will develop into productive action if you are diligent and remain transparent with yourself and with God. You should see a difference as you set the stage to move from rebuilding your mindset to a call-to-action. Your perception helps you make that transition.

Perception is the lens through which you see the world. How you perceive yourself, God, the world, and others paints a picture you will use to respond to others. Perception is extremely important, and that's why the awareness stage of this study makes you keenly aware of how you've been thinking, reacting, and operating all this time. You may even determine that your perception of certain things may need to change. Change is not something to be fearful of but should be embraced. If you are not happy or fulfilled with your current reality, you know changes need to be made. Work on your perception of life and you will change your path in life.

In the space below, write down your perception of your reality, your existence. Explain how you view the world in relation to your existence.

What is My Perception of God, the World, and My Place in the World?

_____
_____
_____
_____
_____
_____
_____
_____
_____
_____
_____
_____
_____
_____

Week 13 – Character

Your character is responsible for your motives, actions, behaviors and beliefs. While you may attain formal knowledge and wealth, character can make you lose all ground you gained in life or it can help you maintain that ground and take you to further heights. Never underestimate the power of your character.

MINDSET: Character shapes us and directs our moral/ethical compass. I am committed to developing my character intentionally with purpose.

LESSON: Character guides our actions and thought process. It is a powerful tool in understanding how far we will progress in life.

Booker T. Washington once said that "character is power." I can't tell you how much truth is contained in this statement. Your character refers to the qualities that make up who you are. It has to do with the moral/ethical qualities that you possess. Have you ever thought about the qualities that make up who you are? Well, now that you're developing the good habit of self-reflecting and understanding who you are, it's important to think about your character. Before moving on to the next quarter, take some time to work on building your character.

Now that you are reprograming your mind, you should confront the behaviors you've displayed up until now. Is it possible that your character or lack thereof has been holding you back? It's time to understand what you've been displaying to others all this time and why.

Use the space below to write down the traits you believe are all a part of your character. Again, you are being vulnerable and honest with yourself, which means you should write down all attributes that you believe are part of your character. Doing so will also help you understand your past actions and behaviors. For example, are you an honorable person? If you saw someone drop money on the ground while standing behind them, would you let the person know, or would you wait until the person leaves and then take the money for yourself? Do you believe in "finders keepers," or do you believe that it's not your money, and since you saw who it belonged to, you should make them aware of what just happened? Your decision and follow-up action can be attributed to your character. So think about those qualities you believe make up your character and write them down below.

As we move into the second quarter and further into the study, you can rebuild your character as understanding continues to flow in your direction. Keep in mind that the goal is to continue learning, *Discerning*, understanding, and developing so that you can make necessary changes and continue to grow as you move forth towards your purpose.

In the space below, write down the attributes of what you believe make up your character.

What Qualities Make up My Character

II. ACTION PLAN
REPENTANCE &
SELF-IMPROVEMENT

WEEKS 14–26

Week 14 – Discipline

Discipline is the catalyst that takes you from the thought of doing something to the physical act of follow-through.

MINDSET: The practice of discipline takes me into a whole new realm of change. Everything is just wishful thinking until I take actual steps towards change. Discipline is the bridge that takes me from mere thought to action.

LESSON: I will learn to live a disciplined life to make better choices and decisions and effectuate positive change in my life. Change starts with discipline.

You now have enough foundational elements for you to begin formulating an action plan that will translate into concrete changes or shifts in your life. After initiating the process of self-analysis, self-awareness, and identification of areas that need attention, you can now enter the stage of developing an action plan. This starts with you making a firm decision to make necessary changes. The first order of business after deciding to change is to learn to be disciplined so changes can be carried out. Discipline is defined as "the practice of training one to obey rules or a code of behavior or to train or develop by instruction and exercise, especially in self-control."[4] This quarter is a study in learning how to become more disciplined as you implement necessary changes that will eventually transform your life.

In the space below, write down the ways in which you need to be more disciplined.

Areas Where I Need to Exercise More Discipline

_____
_____
_____
_____
_____
_____
_____
_____
_____
_____
_____
_____
_____
_____
_____
_____
_____
_____
_____
_____
_____
_____

---

[4] Oxford Dictionary.

Week 15 – Fasting

Fasting is an opportunity to have your mind, heart and senses in alignment with one another. Fasting is an act of spiritual and mental elevation and physical submission. It is also an opportunity to deepen your relationship with God.

MINDSET: I will view fasting not as deprivation but as elevation; not as deprivation, but as a redirection of purpose that will assist me in making healthy changes in life.

LESSON: Fasting is a way to physically express my commitment to God and a true test of my will.

One of the best ways to physically express your act of discipline is through fasting. Fasting is a wonderful practice that you should implement to strengthen your relationship with God. The more you strengthen your relationship with God, the more other areas in your life are strengthened as well. This is no coincidence. Although many people fast to lose weight, the act of fasting in relation to God is so that you can quiet the outside noise and hear the voice of God. Losing weight is a wonderful by-product of your fasting regimen, not the focus. The focus is for you to learn to hear that *Discerning* voice of God. Fasting helps you focus on God and, in turn, helps you understand where you need to focus your efforts and why.

Fasting is not just about turning down food. As you start to think about fasting, think about other areas in your life that you need to bring under control. Perhaps you need to fast from watching certain types of media that influence your mood, or perhaps you need to stop engaging in gossip at work. If change is truly going to occur, fasting is a great place to begin because it leads you down the right path. Incorporate fasting into your study as a life tool that you use consistently. There are a number of books devoted to the concept of spiritual fasting that can help you. First start to look at passages in the Bible that speak on the topic of fasting.[5] Once you identify areas in your life where you need to fast, start to research books that may help you plan how you will commence fasting.[6]

---

[5] For example, see Daniel 9:3 ESV; Matthew 6:18 ESV.
[6] *Fasting for Breakthrough and Deliverance* by John Eckhardt.

Now that you know you can fast in different areas in your life and not just food, in the space below, write down the areas in your life where you need to fast.

Areas in My Life Where I Will Implement Fasting

Week 16 – Obedience

Obedience is often the first test of your character and commitment. Once you learn the value of obedience, you remove the mask of stubbornness as one of your stumbling blocks and begin a new chapter of success.

MINDSET: I will view obedience in relation to my walk with God and simultaneously remove the negative perception of obedience from my mind.

LESSON: Learning to be obedient is a form of discipline that garners positive results. I will use obedience to strengthen my walk with God as I continue to strengthen my mind.

Obedience is often a word used in the negative to imply weakness. But just like the word 'Meek' is misconstrued, the true meaning of obedience carries opportunities to become stronger in mind and body. As you begin fasting, obedience keeps you from giving up. The more you understand that obedience leads you down the road of progress, the more you will understand why obedience is important.

Obedience is not automatically synonymous with suffering; it is about making a decision and staying the course. It is also a deeper understanding of consequences and actions. When you know your obedience is laced with purpose and fulfillment, you will not look back or waver on your commitment. You will instead look forward because your mind will be filled with the proper expectation of what obedience will bring: strength of Will, strength of character, positive change, order, and clarity. These are the thoughts you should be thinking as you embark on fasting. Obedience will keep you in the proper headspace.

Do you struggle with obedience? In the space below, write down why you struggle with obedience.

Reasons Why I Struggle with Obedience

_____
_____
_____
_____
_____
_____
_____
_____
_____
_____
_____
_____
_____
_____
_____
_____
_____
_____
_____

Week 17 – Health

A healthy body starts a ripple effect to different areas of your life that extend far beyond your physical body and can surely result in generational changes. There's a reason why it is often said that health is wealth.

MINDSET: I will work on improving my health by making small, manageable and appropriate changes to my lifestyle one day at a time so that I can maintain a healthy way of life for me and my loved ones.

LESSON: I will educate myself about health in general and my body specifically. I will identify and break away from any bad habits that results in a decline in my health. Discipline is key.

It is no secret that a healthy body moves you in the direction of a healthy mind. But it also moves you in the direction of lifestyle changes that affect you and others. You'll notice that deciding to eat healthier is a form of discipline. It is also a change that makes you understand that you can make changes in other areas of your life. Health is wealth because it can prolong your life. You can then be there for your loved ones longer and make time for other things you weren't able to do before.

In other words, the door is ajar for you to explore new things physically, mentally, emotionally, and of course, spiritually.

In the space below, make two columns. In the first column, write down some of the unhealthy foods you've been eating. In the second column, write down healthier food alternatives that you could use to replace the unhealthy items. This may require you to do some research, but it will be worth it in the end. Remember, you are still exercising discipline. You can do it!

In the space below, write down your health issues and what changes you need to make in order to improve your overall health.

My Health Struggles

_____
_____
_____
_____
_____
_____
_____

1. <u>UHEALTHY FOODS I EAT</u>   2. <u>HEALTHY FOOD ALTERNATIVES</u>

_____
_____
_____
_____
_____
_____
_____

Week 18 – Responsibility

Taking responsibility for your life starts when you accept your role in where you are in your life. No one is completely blame-free in relation to where we find ourselves at any given point in life. As you accept responsibility for your part, you begin to mature in life as well.

MINDSET: I will learn to be more conscious of my thoughts, words, and actions by taking responsibility for the choices I make.

LESSON: As I take responsibility for my life, I will also learn to look more introspectively and, therefore, learn to take accountability for what I do, say, believe, and how I react to others and situations.

Taking responsibility for what you put out in the world and how you respond to others or your circumstances is another significant step in the right direction. It is a clear indication that you are changing for the better. It is also a sign of maturity that will deepen if you continue to work on self and not lay blame on others for undesirable situations in which you find yourself involved. As you continue to mature, you will also be able to avoid those undesirable situations because you will be able to identify them and subsequently avoid them. Once again, taking responsibility fosters discipline because you will learn to resist those temptations that take you into unwanted territory—places you are specifically trying to avoid. You will take more focused steps, and you will know when to move and when to stay put. Remember, you are also praying daily, and you now know that consistent prayer will bring forth clarity in a variety of ways. Taking responsibility for your actions gets you to a higher-level of existence; your learning ability has just increased. In addition, being responsible makes you accountable for what you are doing. So not only will you be responsible in your steps and how you proceed, you will also hold yourself accountable when you do make mistakes so that you take ownership of what you've done. This is maturity in action.

In the space below, write down the ways in which you can be more responsible with your thoughts, words, and actions towards yourself and others.

How I Can Take Responsibility for Me

_____
_____
_____
_____
_____
_____
_____
_____
_____
_____
_____

Week 19 – Commitment

Staying committed is a way of realizing your understanding of the importance of what you are trying to accomplish. When you commit to a task, you are making a pledge that you will follow through.

MINDSET: Commitment is about strengthening my belief system. As I increase my knowledge base of what I believe, I will increase my ability to commit.

LESSON: My commitment is tied to my beliefs and, therefore, I will continue to strengthen my beliefs by strengthening my relationship with God.

Commitment is another way that your character is tested along with your belief system. How strongly do you believe in what you are practicing? If you do not truly believe in what you are doing, then you will not fully commit to the plan of action. Look at how you handled commitment in the past. It is important to narrow down why you did not follow through with your past attempts at taking on projects. Hopefully, what is making the difference between now and then is all you are learning in this study and how your knowledge base is strengthened by facts and substantiated by your results.

The more you continue to work on your character, the more you will be less inclined to give up. You will use all that you learned to make decisions regarding your level of commitment and think it through before you either change course or decide to let something go.

In the space below, write down anything you committed yourself to doing and then went back on the commitment. It could be a commitment to self or others. Why did you stop being committed?

Commitment(s) I Allowed to Fall Through and Why

_____
_____
_____
_____
_____
_____
_____
_____
_____
_____
_____
_____
_____
_____
_____
_____
_____
_____

Week 20 – Confidence

Having confidence is a strong indication of how your mindset is being fed positively and consistently. The more you learn and commit yourself to putting into practice what you've learned, the more confident you will become of your progress and ultimate success.

MINDSET: I will be confident in my walk because I believe in me.

LESSON: My Confidence is increased as I quell the unsubstantiated fear within that is nothing more than outside influences that attempt to rob me of my progress and keep me from my goals.

Confidence is a barometer of how you are progressing. Having confidence does not mean that fear is completely gone, it just means that despite the fear, you know you have what it takes to move forward and succeed. Confidence is a belief in yourself, even if others do not. It is you coming to a crossroads and choosing you over the fear and the objections of others. Confidence is also about you having an intimate knowledge of yourself, your strengths, your weaknesses, and how you handle all of them. The more you understand and work on you, the more confident you will become, and the less you will question your ability to succeed. Confidence starts and ends with you. You must choose you over the fear. The more you continue to learn, the more you will build your confidence.

Have you struggled with confidence in the past? In the space below, write down the ways in which you struggled with confidence. If you can recall why you struggled with confidence in the past, write it down as well.

My Struggle with Confidence

_____
_____
_____
_____
_____
_____
_____
_____
_____
_____
_____
_____
_____
_____
_____
_____
_____
_____

Week 21 – Organization

Nothing clears the mind like organization. Organizing your personal space gives you clarity of purpose and helps you with stuck energy that may interfere with your mental progress.

MINDSET: I will learn to perform a periodic organization check to ensure that I'm not losing momentum or blocking energy from flowing; I chose not to stump my creative ability.

LESSON: Organization helps me increase my mental capacity and ability to think and create more effectively. Organization creates room for more opportunities all around.

Many people underestimate the value of being organized either because they believe they are organized or do not see it as a problem that needs to be addressed. However, physical organization influences your mental faculties. If you are constantly looking through piles of documents, clothes, or various items, you are directing energy away from pertinent areas that will help you plan, create, and execute. Take a good look at your personal space at home and at work and learn the value of purging, organizing, and reorganizing. Within your various piles of clutter, you may find your creativity. To clear the clutter is to clear the mind. Give your mind the space and opportunity it has been looking for by learning to organize your various spaces periodically. You will be surprised how your mind will open up with ideas, creativity, clarity, and purpose.

In the space below, make a list of all the areas in your life that need organization and commit to tackling a different organization project every week.

My Proposed Organization Projects

_____
_____
_____
_____
_____
_____
_____
_____
_____
_____
_____
_____
_____
_____
_____
_____
_____

Week 22 – Strength

Strength refers to spiritual, physical and mental strength. As you work on your body and mind, you will find that you have levels of strength you never had before. Strength is power.

MINDSET: I am strong in mind, body, and spirit and therefore I am capable of strength beyond my wildest dreams.

LESSON: Strength is just as much a state of mind as it is a physical manifestation of health. I will continue to work on my physical and mental strength, which will allow me to increase my strength in every way possible.

Having strength means having the endurance to move forward, to forge ahead, particularly when times become stressful or when roadblocks are in sight. This is why strength should be built consistently and continually as a primary directive before times become challenging. In fact, the whole point of what we are studying is to become strong in will, mind, body and spirit. There is no question that there will be bumps in the road. When that happens, the question becomes: How strong are you to handle a crisis, and will that strength wane during stormy weather? You should continue to build up your strength physically by maintaining good health and mentally by working on self to develop your endurance and toughness internally and externally. When you know God is always rooting for you, it doesn't matter who is against you. Knowing this fact will help you navigate the challenges and focus on the victory.

In what ways are you strong mentally and/or physically? Don't be bashful; write down how strong you are.

My Strengths

Week 23 – Respect

Respect should not be premised on who earned it and who did not. We should all give one another respect based upon the fundamental human principle that we are all human beings, and all human life should be respected.

MINDSET: I will learn to lead with respect because I want to receive respect in return.

LESSON: I will not allow others' negative dispositions dictate whether or not I give respect. To do so allows others to control my actions and dictate outcomes that are inconsistent with my goals.

The popular saying about respect is that it is to be earned. That is not true; this is also why there are so many problems with human interaction. We should all give respect because we all want to be respected. We should all respect one another because we are all human. End of story. This is a basic principle that many of us fail to grasp. However, at this time in your study of this book, you should be progressing in understanding your purpose and goals. One of those understandings should be that withholding respect based upon your subjective standard as to whether someone "earned" your respect or not, will only lead to conflict and loss of control. After twenty-two weeks of study, that is not where we want to be. In fact, that mentality actually negates what we learned.

Again, we are not operating under man's standard of living; we are operating under God's standard. To do so means that we look to his standard of how to treat one another, and that means treating all human life with respect. When we deviate from the Godly standard, we get off course and run the risk of creating unnecessary circumstances that may have lasting consequences that impede our progress. Remember the commitment, the strength, the confidence, and all the work you've done so far to stay on course. You've come too far to allow someone else's actions derail all your work and progress. Respect is part of your action plan that you will continue to execute even when others you encounter do not reciprocate. Another's belief system should not shake your belief system. You have a heightened sense of awareness that will help you maintain your present course. Don't lose sight of these facts.

What is your view of respect? Write it down on the lines below.

My View of Respect

_____
_____
_____
_____
_____
_____
_____
_____
_____
_____

Week 24 - Ethics

Ethics is a set of principles that you stand upon. These principles shape your belief system and behavior. When you have principles that you believe in, you now have standards in which to make proper decisions; decisions that are in alignment with these ethical principles.

MINDSET: Ethics sets the tone for what I will accept in my life and what I will not accept.

LESSON: Ethics act as boundary lines to ensure that I'm walking in accordance with my belief system. Others are placed on notice as a result of my ethics.

This is the perfect opportunity for you to start implementing standards that you believe align with your moral standards. Ethics is either the philosophy or the written code of conduct you live by. Ethics act as an additional protector, guidance and boundary line that serves the purpose of safeguarding you from unnecessary situations that threaten your progress. Learn to set ethical standards and stick to them. You may work in a profession that upholds ethical standards. If so, take a look at them and then think about the ethical standards you uphold personally. As you continue to learn about and hear the *Discerning* voice of God, your ethical standards will become clear.

In the space provided, write down the ethical standards you currently live by.

My Ethical Standards

_____
_____
_____
_____
_____
_____
_____
_____
_____
_____
_____
_____
_____
_____
_____
_____
_____
_____
_____
_____

Week 25 – Integrity

Your integrity is one of the moral and ethical standards that you live by and use to stand tall. It is the cornerstone of honesty and truthfulness.

MINDSET: My integrity is a foundational element that will stand the test of time. I will continue to stand on my integrity by standing firm on truth and honesty.

LESSON: Standing on integrity will oftentimes be my saving grace when I have to make difficult decisions in life. Learning to stand firm on integrity will assist me in making better decisions because I will be clear about which way to go.

Integrity is that moral voice inside you that leads both in times of clarity and uncertainty. It is one of those ethical standards we discussed last week. However, most of us do not think of our integrity until we are faced with adversity or a tough decision that calls into question our integrity. If you lack integrity, you need to ask yourself why. Your moral values need to be built on integrity, honor, and strength. Integrity is also rooted in responsibility, honesty, and accountability. If you are having trouble in this area or if your past includes a history of dishonesty, a sense of entitlement, or other ways in which you've gotten ahead other than through hard and honest work, dig deeper to understand why.

Now is the time to work in this area. It will not be easy, but you will need to work harder on your belief system. The self-reflection area needs to strike at the heart of why you believe what you believe and how you can change that belief system for the better. Continue to work in this area as needed. Your integrity will precede you. This area will spring forth an abundance of growth and allow you to attract the type of people you need in your life. Integrity leads to truth.

Is integrity important to you? What is your view of integrity? Write it down in the space below.

My Definition of Integrity

Week 26 – Honor

Integrity leads to honor. It keeps you in a position of moral responsibility because you are committed to holding yourself to a standard of living that will always hold you accountable no matter the situation you are facing.

MINDSET: I hold myself in high regard because I stand on honor. My honor is derived from my integrity and always guides my moral compass.

LESSON: Honor is a first cousin of integrity and respect that works together like a well-oiled machine. It is the trifecta that will always keep my mental strength in line because I hold my life and purpose in great esteem.

Honor is certainly holding yourself in great esteem, but it is not prideful. Let's make that distinction right now. Honor is the end product of the integrity, respect, and strength you built up all this time. But here is an extremely important part about honor: although it is the act of you holding yourself in high regard, it is not boastful because it is not rooted in pride. On the contrary, honor is rooted in truth. This is why you want to stand in honor; it incorporates the quality of humility that we worked on earlier in the study. You can stand firm on honor because it continues to shape your character on solid ground. Commit to standing on honor in every area of your life.

Can you think of ways in which you've upheld honor either for yourself, your family, or your country? In the space below, list any ways you believe you uphold honor.

My Stance on Honor

_____
_____
_____
_____
_____
_____
_____
_____
_____
_____
_____
_____
_____
_____
_____
_____
_____
_____
_____
_____
_____
_____

III. LIGHT
Enlightenment

Weeks 27–39

Week 27 – Openness

Being open creates opportunities in many areas. It opens up the mind and heart for healing, acceptance and a willingness to work with others.

MINDSET: As I continue to work on myself, I remain open to all the possibilities that God has set before me.

LESSON: Openness leads to opportunities for me to learn, grow, and expand my territory.

We start the third quarter off with the quality of openness because we are entering enlightenment. We started the first quarter with self-awareness, proceeded with our action plan, and we should have learned enough for us to begin expanding our reach by thinking and working with others. The first step after working on ourselves is to realize that we were not placed on this earth to focus solely on ourselves. We grow through collaboration. We also understand that we do not have all the answers ourselves. Therefore, it is important for us to remain open so that God can place us in areas of need. As you learn to *Discern* more, you will know when to get involved and make a difference. With God involved in the process, you will remain open to see where you are going and what encounters God will lead you to that will open doors you thought were previously closed to you.

Do you have trouble being open? In what ways do you struggle with openness? What is the cause of this struggle? Go back as far as you need to in order to determine the root of the struggle.

My Struggle with Being Open

_____
_____
_____
_____
_____
_____
_____
_____
_____
_____
_____
_____
_____
_____
_____
_____
_____
_____
_____
_____
_____
_____

Week 28 – Appreciation

Appreciation starts with you learning to appreciate who you are, where you are and what you are trying to accomplish. Your appreciation of yourself will cause you to appreciate life in general and allow you to appreciate circumstances and others as life lessons, not hinderances.

MINDSET: I will learn to appreciate me and my life—my shortcomings as well as my good qualities. The more I appreciate myself, the more I will appreciate others and place situations I face in proper perspective.

LESSON: Appreciation leads to acceptance and gratitude.

Appreciation is a blessing in disguise. As with anything, you must appreciate yourself before you can appreciate others or even situations. When you learn to appreciate yourself, you also learn to accept yourself. Appreciating yourself means you are aware that God made you the way you are for a reason. You have a uniqueness about you that no one else can duplicate. You will also realize that you were never meant to be like someone else.

But one of the most important aspects of appreciation is that you can appreciate your shortcomings just as much as your strong points. You appreciate those shortcomings because they should be used as a training ground for improvement, not regret or self-pity. Appreciation makes you aware that we all have things to work on, and that's how we learn. But just because we are learning, it does not mean we cannot appreciate who we are, what we have accomplished, what we're working towards, and what we've learned along the way. Beating up on ourselves is not the way to go. The more you appreciate you, the more you learn to be open with yourself about your progress and where you need to go.

What have you learned to appreciate about yourself? Write it down in the space below.

Why I Appreciate Me

_____
_____
_____
_____
_____
_____
_____
_____
_____
_____
_____
_____
_____

Week 29 – Guidance

Allowing God's guidance in your life is not only appropriate, it is necessary. This is the guidance you have been waiting for all this time; the guidance that will never steer you wrong and will place you exactly where you need to be.

MINDSET: I will be open to God's guidance and instruction in my life to ensure that my steps are purposeful and necessary.

LESSON: God knows what I'm supposed to be doing, so allowing his guidance to foster my steps will take me farther than I ever imagined and take me places I never thought I'd be.

Depending upon what you've identified as things you must manage or work on, it may be difficult to imagine giving up control by allowing God to be at the helm of your decisions. But if you are making strides in your progress with self, you know that you're not in control; God is in control. This is the time to let go of the control you think you have, keep that stubborn nature of yours at bay, and allow God to work his magic in you so you can be more effective for yourself and others. While we really should allow God's guidance in our lives immediately, we discuss it now because we first need to understand how we've been operating and the ways in which we've been sabotaging our progress in life. As we continue to deepen our relationship with God, we become 'enlightened' because we now understand that he is in control and we need to stop trying to control everything.

At this point, your learning meter is high, so you are ready to take your gifts to the next level by understanding your role and God's role. Allowing God to mold your steps strengthens the relationship and exposes you to even greater opportunities in life. That willingness to be open is the bridge to allowing God to guide your steps. Don't stop now; the journey is just beginning.

Are you a controlling person? What areas in your life do you need to let go and let God? Write it down in the space below.

Areas in My Life That I Need to Let Go of Control

___
___
___
___
___
___
___
___
___
___
___
___
___
___
___
___

Week 30 – Courage

Courage is the ability to step away from the fear and actually move forward anyway. Courage is the physical manifestation of your confidence. It is a mental state of knowing over feeling and execution. The display of courage comes from learning that deep inside you have the power within to push through and succeed.

MINDSET: God gave me the courage to endure, persevere, and to change. Therefore, I have nothing to fear with God guiding my steps.

LESSON: My mental strength has been built for courage. God will never take me places I can't handle. Courage is the physical manifestation of my confidence.

Your mind is now stronger than it was when you initially started this study. While any fear you have will not be totally gone, fear will take a back seat to your courage. Remember the cowardly lion in *The Wizard of Oz*? If so, then you will also remember that although he had other attributes and a desire to help, he could not move forward because he did not possess courage. Courage is the catalyst that will make you move forward. Imagine having all the tools necessary to make a difference in the world but unable to move due to lack of courage. God's involvement in your life stops this scenario from happening. Now that God has taken his rightful place in your life, it's time to release the courage inside you. God will reveal to you what has been holding you back all this time. And if that revelation calls for you to step away from someone, it may seem scary. This is true especially if it is someone you've placed your trust in for years. But if you continue to rely upon God for instruction and not give into your fears, you will discover the courage to make the right decision and then move forward with action.

How has your courage increased since allowing God's Divine Guidance in your life? Write it down in the space below.

Specific Areas in Life Where I've Gained Courage

Week 31 – Trust

Trust is putting your confidence and your complete belief in someone. It is giving someone access to you and allowing your life to be influenced by another.

MINDSET: I trust God completely to give me all that I need in order to succeed in life.

LESSON: I will learn to trust God in all areas of my life, not just in certain areas.

Often, we have problems with trust because someone may have betrayed our trust. On an even bigger scale, we may have blamed God for allowing someone else to betray our trust. We must now purge ourselves of these thoughts and consider any prior betrayals from others as learning lessons. We learned earlier that we must take responsibility for those situations we allowed ourselves to become involved in without looking to blame. We are way past the blame game. We are in a period of enlightenment and we will not look back.

The truth is, if we allowed God to guide us a long time ago, we would have avoided a lot of pain and suffering that we experienced. It's time to place our full trust in God. In fact, it's way overdue.

Have you had issues with trust in the past? Write down any situations that diminished your ability to trust.

My Issues with Trust

___

Week 32 – Faith

Faith is akin to trust in that once you give someone your complete trust, you must have faith that the person will do what you expect them to do with that trust."

MINDSET: I trust God and, therefore, I have faith that God will always come through with my best interests at heart.

LESSON: Trust and faith go hand and hand. I cannot fully have faith in God if I do not fully trust God. Therefore, I will trust and have faith in God completely.

You cannot say you have faith in God and not fully trust him. This is why we work on trust the week prior to dealing with faith. Let's put it this way: Trust is the declaration that you believe in God and faith is putting your money where your mouth is. So, in other words, stop worrying. You can't say you believe in God's authority in your life, seek his guidance, and then continue to worry about the same things you placed in God's hands. It doesn't work that way. You're either in, or you're out. You cannot have it both ways when it comes to God. If this is an area you've struggled with in the past, go back to your notes and continue to identify and work on your issues of trust and faith so you will continue to get stronger in your walk with God. Believe me, you've got what it takes. Don't allow others who may have betrayed your trust to stop you from trusting and placing your faith in God.

Have you placed your faith in God? What is stopping you from doing so? Write down any areas in your life that have made you question your faith.

Faith and Me: Why I Struggle with Faith

_____
_____
_____
_____
_____
_____
_____
_____
_____
_____
_____
_____
_____
_____
_____
_____
_____
_____
_____
_____

Week 33 – Understanding

Understanding is one of the foundational elements of selflessness. You begin with an understanding of God, an understanding of self, and then you can begin to understand others. You can understand others when you comprehend that another's situation is different from yours. Understanding is an important factor in your growth and development.

MINDSET: I will seek to attain understanding in all that I do by asking God to guide my steps and help me to grasp the broader concept of understanding beyond my situation and myself.

LESSON: Understanding leads to compassion, collaboration, community, and growth.

The more you learn, grow, and realize that you were not meant to just work a job, eat, sleep, and get into a daily routine that doesn't lead to any fulfillment, the more you begin to break out of that mode of selfishness. Your life was meant to add value to others. God knew this all along, of course. God did not put you here to focus on selfish wants. However, it's only when you understand what you've been doing and get to a point where you identify what needs to change within that you will realize your life means so much more than an unexamined routine. Your understanding of the world and your part in it will be realized and guided by God. Remember, allow yourself to be guided by God. Trust God. Have faith in God. By doing this, you will learn to understand God more fluidly. Your understanding of God will spill over into you understanding others. Understanding doesn't mean you accept or adopt another's disposition as your own, it means that you acknowledge how others are different from you, have different points of view and have different circumstances to overcome. Understanding is a form of appreciation that allows you to appreciate another's plight and value outside of your own.

What are the ways you can understand others in your life, such as those you work with or people in your life? What differences have you come across that you can stand to appreciate better? Write it down in the space below.

Areas in Which I Stand to Gain a Better Understanding of Others

_____
_____
_____
_____
_____
_____
_____
_____
_____
_____

Week 34 – Compassion

Compassion for others begins when you start to understand that there are others experiencing different struggles from you with different and, in many instances, even more dire situations. Having compassion for others means you understand that you are not the only one experiencing many hardships in life. Compassion requires us to do better at understanding one another.

MINDSET: I can still have compassion for others while working on myself; the two are not mutually exclusive. There is room for understanding that extends beyond my circumstances.

LESSON: Understanding leads to compassion for others. Compassion does not mean that I place others above my needs. It just means that I make room in my heart for others.

Compassion sets in as your level of understanding increases. Compassion starts the process for you to see life on a deeper level. It is an enlightening moment when you can see beyond your situation and have compassion for others' plight in life. Often, we are caught up in the belief that our struggles are unlike anyone else's struggles. Or we believe that our situation is worse than anyone else's situation. Both beliefs are simply not true. We spend too much time trying to convince ourselves and others that our pain is greater than all others. This should never be our focus. But more importantly, the more you grow and mature, the more you will understand that the struggle is <u>NOT</u> about who's pain is greater. In our natural selfish state, we all think our pain is greater than anyone else's pain. Do you see how problematic that is? It all comes back to our selfishness.

When we learn to stop focusing on ourselves, we can learn the value of working on ourselves and helping others. Compassion helps us see that disposition more clearly, and we need to learn to be more compassionate. As we gain a better understanding of ourselves, our surroundings, and people in general, we learn to have more compassion for others. Having compassion for others means you must learn to be less selfish and have more concern for others. We all stand to shed our inherent selfishness. Being selfish always gets us into trouble.

Do you have compassion for others? In what ways have you shown your compassion for others? Write it down in the space below.

Ways in Which I Feel Compassion for Others

_____
_____
_____
_____
_____
_____
_____
_____
_____
_____
_____
_____
_____
_____
_____
_____
_____
_____
_____
_____
_____
_____
_____

Week 35 – Empathy

Empathy brings us to an even deeper level of understanding as we deal with people on a more personal level by acquiring specific knowledge of a person's pain and struggle and learning to acknowledge and respect it.

MINDSET: I will seek to gain a deeper understanding of one's struggles and thereby deepen the human connection between myself and others.

LESSON: Empathy is a deeper level of compassion that helps me better understand human suffering as well as human strength.

Empathy takes that general compassion for people and narrows it to particular persons and individual struggles. This is about as close as you can get to placing yourself in someone else's shoes. This is not about you sacrificing yourself for every unfortunate situation of another that you encounter. It is still about understanding. It is understanding human suffering on a deeper, more personal level that positions you to help others from God's point of view.

Can you think of instances where you empathized with another? What made you feel this way? How did this help you understand the person better? Write it down in the space below.

Times When I Had Empathy for Others

Week 36 – Happiness

Happiness is also a state of mind. Happiness cannot be found in someone else. It starts from within and illuminates to others on the outside.

MINDSET: I will seek happiness from within because I am happy with the person I am and who God made me to be.

LESSON: Happiness is not premised on material things; it is a disposition, a state of mind.

There are many of us walking around trying to find happiness externally. This is a huge mistake. No one else can give you happiness but you. It does not matter how many shopping sprees, cocktails, shoes, cars, or other material items you may acquire. If you feel emptiness or loneliness despite all the material items you have, then you need to understand why you feel such emptiness and unfulfillment. Happiness comes from a realization that you are enough; it is the firm belief that you are where you are supposed to be and that you have everything you need in life.

If we attach our happiness to someone else or something else, then we start to have problems. You must ask yourself why you believe happiness has been elusive for you. As you continue to self-reflect, you should take quiet time with yourself to confront your issues of happiness. As your relationship with God grows stronger, God will remove obstacles, including people, that you could not remove yourself. The mental stress that has blocked your sense of happiness will disappear. The more you trust in God, the happier you will become, and you will find that your happiness has been in front of you all along. When you are happy, you can be happy for others. Happiness is contagious. It's time for you to claim your happiness.

Are you happy? Why or why not? Write in the space below what or who you've connected your happiness to. Can you identify what makes you happy?

What Do You Believe You Lack That Affects Your Happiness? If You Believe You are Happy, What Makes You Happy?

_____
_____
_____
_____
_____
_____
_____
_____
_____
_____
_____
_____
_____
_____
_____

Week 37 – Community

Community is how we grow. We cannot learn and grow if we only rely upon self-knowledge and think we have all the answers to life's problems. We have much to learn from others' stories and experiences. We build upon what we learn from others to find common ground as we expand our understanding of the human condition.

MINDSET: I will learn the value of community and know that as I follow God's direction, God will place people in my life for specific reasons, and I will trust God's decisions.

LESSON: No man is an island. I was not meant to be isolated. Relationships are of great value, and I will learn to form relationships wisely and build a community.

Having the ability to form relationships is how we connect and grow. If you have consistent trouble forming lasting relationships, now is the time to figure out why. The notion that you will go it alone in this world will not get you very far. There is an African Proverb that states: *'If you want to go fast, go alone; but if you want to go far, go together.'* We were not meant to roam the earth alone. Often, the problems we are having with others and the unpleasant situations we find ourselves in may be caused by ourselves. Creating a community is a significant part of our development. God will direct our steps in the direction of the right people whether it's for a lesson or a reward. As we interact with others, keeping in mind his purpose, we will grow in community and also grow individually.

Have you had trouble forming relationships? Write down in the space below any barriers you believe have impeded your ability to form relationships.

My Ability to Form Relationships and Build a Community- How Effective am I with Forming Relationships?

_____
_____
_____
_____
_____
_____
_____
_____
_____
_____
_____
_____
_____
_____
_____

Week 38 – Objectivity

The ability to look at things objectively is a strong sign of growth and maturity. Being able to look at people and situations objectively provides a basis for you to Discern consistently.

MINDSET: I will learn to see things more objectively to gain the full picture of what is being presented before me.

LESSON: Looking at situations and information objectively means that I look at facts and not allow my feelings or other distractors to take control of my rational thinking.

Your hard work is starting to pay off. The truth of the matter is that God gave us emotions along with other qualities for a reason. However, emotions can run amok if we allow them to cloud our sense of reason. Also, when we are acting selfishly, we tend to see things from our selfish perspective; such a perspective is filled with emotions. But as we grow in our walk with God, we begin to see a different picture presented from God's point of view, not our own and not someone else's picture. That ability to see things in a different, more healthy way is you tapping more into that *Discerning* voice of God. This is you sifting through all information and extracting the salient pieces of information that hold the keys to how you need to proceed.

This does not mean your emotions are irrelevant. On the contrary, emotions are valuable; you just need to know when to act upon them and when to put them to the side. Learning to *Discern* is one of your greatest abilities to navigate the various pitfalls in life. God gives us that ability, and as you become closer to God, your ability to *Discern* will sharpen and grow. Learning to see both sides of the coin is the litmus test. If you can do that, you are maturing, growing, and headed in the right direction.

Can you look at things objectively, or do you allow emotions to cloud your judgment? Write down whether you primarily act based upon emotions, or by using facts. Explain why.

My Primary Basis for Making Decisions: Emotions or Facts?

_____
_____
_____
_____
_____
_____
_____
_____
_____
_____
_____
_____
_____
_____

Week 39 – Empowerment

*The more you know and learn, the more you grow.
Knowledge is power; knowledge breeds empowerment.
The feeling of empowerment is a feeling of confidence in
self and a confirmation of what you know to be true.*

MINDSET: I am empowered because I believe in me. God has given me the authority to proceed through the feeling of empowerment.

LESSON: Empowerment is self-autonomy and strength of character.

Empowerment means your belief in yourself has taken on a new level, which will translate into action. Not only do you believe you can do something, you now *know* you can do it. We worked on empowerment in this last week of the enlightenment phase because it leads you right into the phase of transformation. In other words, it is the place you want to be in order to move from believing to knowing and then to actually doing. You already have the confidence and courage; empowerment is an extension of what you know to be true. It is action transforming into realization. You should feel empowered to make your goals and carry them through. Empowerment will spill over in other areas in your life and help you mobilize effectively. Empowerment is internal power translated into external power. You are ready to take on a leadership role. And remember, since you are already working on discipline, you are in a position to move from thought to action. You have the courage to physically move forward and you are empowered with the knowledge to do so effectively. What a powerful combination!

How do you feel empowered in your life? Write it down in the space below.

My Road to Empowerment

_____
_____
_____
_____
_____
_____
_____
_____
_____
_____
_____
_____
_____
_____
_____
_____
_____
_____

IV. Transformation Change
Weeks 40–52

Week 40 – Selflessness

Selflessness is the pivotal point in life when you unequivocally understand that life is not always about you. It is the awakening of your spiritual self that puts you in touch with your gifts and talents to be glorified for the greater good, not for selfish gain.

MINDSET: My life is far more than satisfying selfish desires.

LESSON: Selfishness leads to a life of untapped potential and stumped growth; my life is worth so much more.

In the book *A Yearn to Discern: Finding Purpose and Fulfillment Through Discernment*, I discuss the dangers of selfishness and how being selfish is really a burden in disguise. We all begin life as selfish people. However, when selfish children continue their selfishness in adulthood, they never win. Selfish people are never satisfied because they are only focused on wants and seek to satisfy their temporary circumstances. They stay in the present without regard for the past or the future. In the end, selfish people are going around in circles while thinking they are getting ahead. Their examination of self is either non-existent or extremely shallow. Unless they engage in deep self-examination and see beyond themselves, their path is a limited one.

However, selfless behavior is premised upon a deeper understanding of yourself and your place in the world. Talents and gifts of the selfless reach a wider audience with benefits that will make you feel complete, motivated, and fulfilled. When you experience the feeling of selflessness, you will begin to wonder why you didn't understand it before, and your selfish ways will be a distant memory that you will not revisit very often.

In what ways have you stopped being selfish and adopted a more selfless attitude? Write down your selfless ways in the space below.

My Progression to Selflessness

Week 41 – Maturity

A mature person is one who maintains an exceptional level of good judgement formed through the focused use of knowledge and experience that is neither boastful nor prideful, but humble and Discerning.

MINDSET: I will use knowledge and experience for purposes of maturity and usefulness according to God's plan.

LESSON: I become mature not just through the acquisition of knowledge, but from the absorption and usefulness of the knowledge I acquire.

Maturity does not come to us because of what comes our way; it comes from the productive use of what we learned. We all have the opportunity to mature, but not all of us accept this responsibility. Maturity is for the committed, the dedicated, the prudent, and the levelheaded person. If we are maturing, that means God is keenly involved in our lives. Maturity takes place as your life transforms. As you continue to acquire new information, it sparks productivity and motivates you to use it wisely. As you mature, your ability to *Discern* is springing forth into action.

Can you see the different ways you have matured over the years and particularly during this year? Write down how much you have matured over the years.

How I Have Matured

Week 42 – Truth

*To know God is to know that there is only one truth.
Truth solidifies a keen sense of right, wrong, ethics
and morality and flows directly from God.*

MINDSET: I will seek truth through God, the one from whom truth is revealed.

LESSON: Seeking truth is my goal because it is through truth that God will move me for his purpose.

It always amazes me when I hear someone say, "I will speak my truth." What they really mean is that they will give their perspective or recite their story. There is a significant difference between speaking your voice and speaking the truth. With that close relationship with God comes the understanding that there is only one truth. There are no "multiple truths." The truth lies with God because he is the originator of truth. And we now know that God reveals truth to us according to his Will. Therefore, we rely upon God's guidance in knowing truth and not our own understanding of truth. How we interpret people, occurrences, situations, and the like, is colored by our experiences, our character, our core, and other influences that we allow into our lives. Therefore, our experiences and knowledge do not automatically translate into us knowing the truth. The gift of truth can only be given to us by God, and truth applies to one and all.

What Truth Has God Revealed to You? How is This Truth Different from What You Believed in the Past? Write it down in the space below.

Week 43 – Wisdom

Wisdom begets Discernment. Wisdom is an extension of maturity that allows your good judgment to be realized through good works.

MINDSET: I will continue to mature in my walk with God to gain Wisdom in all that God has in store for me.

LESSON: Wisdom is *Discernment* in action.

All my life, I heard the popular saying: "Wisdom comes with age." I thought this meant the older you get, the more you automatically gain wisdom. However, I eventually learned that wisdom comes from God, and not everyone gains wisdom as they grow older. Even though opportunities for all of us to attain wisdom is there, wisdom is not bestowed upon everyone. Wisdom can only penetrate your mind if you reprogram your mind, as we discussed at the beginning of this book. All of the studying, understanding, praying, learning to hear the *Discerning* voice of God, maturity, vision, and complete focus on God results in productive change, which translates into action. When those actions are performed, they will be done so with wisdom. Waiting for wisdom to come as you age is not a good idea. Wisdom requires good and necessary work by walking with God. There is nothing automatic about it.

Write Down Your Beliefs about Wisdom. How Has Attaining Wisdom Changed Your Life?

Week 44 – Vision

As it relates to you reaching your goals and moving towards your purpose, your vision is determined by your capacity to use your past appropriately, see beyond your present circumstances and focus on the broader picture including your future. Vision leads you to Hope.

MINDSET: My vision is what keeps me focused on the end game; this includes focusing on where I am going and how I'm getting to my destination.

LESSON: Vision keeps me focused.

Vision is not only about your ability to see with your eyes; it is also about your ability to see with your mind. A renewing of the mind calls for a renewing of vision. You are going from walking your path to walking your path under God's guidance. The difference should be clear to you. Vision takes into account the past, present, and future. It also includes your peripheral vision, which is usually where the dangers are hidden. Going from thinking only about yourself to thinking about yourself and others allows you to see the complete vision more than before. Vision also helps you avoid getting back into the pitfall of focusing on your immediate situation or temporary setbacks. Vision is a form of discipline that keeps you on the road to victory.

What is your vision for the future? How has God changed your vision from when you first began this study? Write down what has changed and where you are headed.

My Vision

Week 45 – Decisiveness

Decisiveness comes with confidence and vision. As God makes the path clear to you, your decisions will be decisive and focused.

MINDSET: I will not be afraid to make decisive decisions because I am confident in my steps and solid in my faith in God.

LESSON: I will not question the path God has set before me. Instead, I will step forward into action decisively with confidence, courage, and strength.

Long gone will be the days of questioning yourself and your steps. Your closeness to God will guide your steps, and you will learn to trust where God is taking you even when he has not revealed every single detail at a given time. The strength of your relationship with God will ignite the trust and faith that you place in God, especially when times are rough. Your decisiveness is the culmination of that relationship and you will continue to move forward with God's blessing and favor.

Take note of the decisiveness of your decisions. Can you see the difference in your decision-making ability now as opposed to in the past? Write down how your decision-making ability has advanced.

How I've Become More Decisive in My Decision-Making Ability

Week 46 – Service

Service is where we want to be. Our gifts, talents and abilities are used to glorify God through service to others. Through service we continue to learn and grow. We increase our level of understanding and our capacity to reach others through service.

MINDSET: I will have an attitude of gratitude through service and glorifying God.

LESSON: My service will sustain me in every way and will increase my capacity to handle more of God's work.

Service is the expression of your love for God. It is through service that we continue to grow as we use our talents, abilities, and gifts by continuing to put them to good, productive use. We grow in community with others, but we also continue to personally grow and develop in the process. Service gives us the opportunity for deeper human understanding as we encounter different people with different circumstances that are unique from ours. Our fruitfulness, territory, and reach are multiplied through service. We continue to serve as God continues to increase our capacity in every way.

How has service opened your eyes? What have you learned through service? Write down the ways in which you've served to glorify God.

My Service

Week 47 – Fairness & Equality

Not only will my decisions be decisive, but they will also be rooted in fairness and equality because commitment to service shapes my understanding of fairness & equality from God's point of view.

MINDSET: My belief in fairness and equality is grounded in my ethics and manifested through my actions with others.

LESSON: I will walk with a cheerful heart and a spirit of fairness and equality for all, not a chosen few.

The stronghold of selfishness is not able to continue its grip on you as you grow in community and faith. The concept of fairness and equality are not just distant concepts but become part of your values and ethical standards. Serving God brings these concepts in sharp focus the more you continue to serve and trust in him.

Write down in the space below how you implement the concepts of fairness and equality in your life.

My Belief in Fairness & Equality

_____
_____
_____
_____
_____
_____
_____
_____
_____
_____
_____
_____
_____
_____
_____
_____
_____
_____
_____
_____
_____
_____
_____
_____
_____

Week 48 – Inner Peace

Although it may have begun with an enormous amount of uncertainty and fear, your continued faithfulness to God brings you to an inner peace and joy that is indescribable and cannot be duplicated by man.

MINDSET: Inner peace comes from within and grows along with my continued faith and trust in God.

LESSON: Inner peace is a consequence of my commitment and strength in God that is lasting and fulfilling.

Inner peace is a lasting quality that comes from the level of commitment, faith, and trust you place in God. The more you trust in God, the more at peace you will be. You will not succumb to worry or fear because you know better, for you cannot trust God and worry at the same time. The strength of your walk with God is a testament to that inner peace and undeniable joy that you feel daily and display to others but, perhaps, could not explain…until now.

In what ways have you found inner peace as you placed your faith and trust in God?

How I Have Achieved Inner Peace

Week 49 – Discernment

Having the ability to sift through different types of information, constant adversity and potential threats in life while consistently making appropriate choices, rational judgments and proper decisions that will propel you forward with the steadfast purpose of improving one's life and ultimately improving the world around you.

MINDSET: The true intent of *Discernment* is to keep you and your actions in alignment with your ultimate purpose in life according to God's Will.

LESSON: *Discernment* is forward-moving and forward-thinking.

All that you learned and the discipline you've displayed over this past year is designed to strengthen your relationship with God so that you can hear the *Discerning* voice of God as you move closer to your true purpose. You will not come out of this study knowing everything. However, God will continue to reveal things to you as you continue to walk with him.

This study is a lifelong study; developing your ability to *Discern* is that gift from God that becomes heightened and more meaningful as threats in life jeopardize your progress. *Discernment* keeps you on course and guides you through the good days and the bad. The goal is to continue *Discerning* as you increase your capacity to glorify God and live out your true purpose. *Discernment* is critical. In the book *A Yearn to Discern: Finding Purpose and Fulfillment Through Discernment*, I use various lessons and exercises in order to gain a keen understanding of the value and power of *Discernment*. It is the mother of all navigation systems that was given to you by God.

What have you learned about *Discernment*? Write down the ways in which your ability to *Discern* has been enhanced through your walk with God.

What I've Learned about My Ability to Discern

_____
_____
_____
_____
_____
_____
_____
_____
_____
_____
_____
_____
_____
_____
_____
_____
_____

Week 50 – Purpose

Discernment leads you to your purpose because your ability to Discern comes from God and increases as you are committed in your walk with God.

MINDSET: Understanding my purpose is connected to my relationship with God and realized through my ability to *Discern*.

LESSON: *Discernment* leads to true purpose according to God's Divine Will.

Many of us spend enormous amounts of time trying to find our purpose in life but can't seem to find it. We allow any and every influence into our lives except the one influence who knows your true intended purpose: God. Knowing your purpose in life is paramount to fulfillment and longevity. Everything we need to fulfill our purpose is within each of us, but we'll never tap into it unless we take the time to reestablish and maintain our relationship with God. Having an intimate relationship with God allows you to hear the *Discerning* voice of God, which guides your steps and leads you to your purpose. Through the process, you learn to build character, stay focused, and continue to grow and learn. Clarity sets in, and the road to your unique purpose will be revealed. You must let go and let God.

Have you discovered your true purpose? Explain how and when God guided you to your purpose in life.

My Purpose in Life

Week 51 – Love

Love conquers all because it breaks all barriers and heals all wounds. Love comes from God; loving God is our first and greatest commandment. When we love God, we are able to love others, including ourselves. Without love, we cannot accomplish anything productive or lasting.

MINDSET: Love removes all limitations and barriers in life.

LESSON: Love is displayed through my actions, not words.

Love builds bridges. Love heals, unites, releases, softens, soothes, and conquers all. There is nothing that love cannot accomplish. We must start with a love of God and a love of self. Love must come first, and it must be an active partner in all that you do. We discuss love in Week 51 simply because sometimes we must uncover all the issues that have stopped us from understanding what love truly is. You cannot expect someone to love themselves and others if they don't know what love is. This is also why we discuss self-love in the beginning of the study. We need to know that God love us and how to love on ourselves before understanding what it means to love others. Once we see how far we were away from love, we can see what love is and how love will change us at our core. When love is at the forefront of all you do, your possibilities are endless, and your imagination knows no boundaries. Love is most definitely the way.

Love is action. In what ways do you show love to God, yourself, and others? Write it down below.

How I Display Love on a Daily Basis

_____
_____
_____
_____
_____
_____
_____
_____
_____
_____
_____
_____
_____
_____
_____
_____
_____
_____
_____
_____
_____
_____
_____

Week 52 – Hope

The understanding of true love and putting love into practice continually leaves us in a state of hope. Hope is that perpetual optimistic view that keeps the spirit lifted and your expectations positive, no matter the situation you face. Hope brings us to the next level of completeness because its foundation is firmly sealed in love.

MINDSET: Hope is a joyful disposition that leads to an optimistic view that is stronger than the world and its problems.

LESSON: Hope is the unwavering belief that good will overcome evil.

If love is in your heart, hope will be the last thought to end your day and the last thought that concludes your actions. Hope calms us because it is a warm feeling that cleanses our perspective to see a brighter future. We continue to have hope even if our current state is in shambles. Do you know why? Because our hope is always beside us. The elements of love, faith, and trust work together to keep hope on standby, elevated far above our circumstances. Hope starts with you but affects others. Hope has the potential to echo into areas we've never been and will stay around long after we are gone.

We end the study with hope because love and hope should be the last feelings we have at the end of our day. If we continue to study, work on ourselves, and place God first, hope will never be a fleeting moment but a tangible reality. Hope will transform you. I will end this study with these final words taken from *A Yearn to Discern*: *Finding Purpose and Fulfillment Through Discernment*:

> *"We need to understand that many times hope is all we have. If we don't have hope, then we allow ourselves a cowardly 'out' when faced with difficult situations that require us to have more courage and faith. The possibility of hope should not only come up when we are in trouble. Hope should be beside you in life at all times like a tried and true friend. We don't always know when we'll need to rely on hope but if it is in the back of our minds as we walk this earth, we can find the good in situations where we didn't think it was possible. It also keeps you in a positive frame of mind when the storms are threatening you and the hail is coming down hard on you. This is why as you Discern in life, the concept of hope should always be a part of the equation as you attempt to improve upon your existence in this world. The value of Hope and Discernment propels you to the highest level of conscious thinking and reasoning."*

- EXCERPT FROM *A YEARN TO DISCERN*

Is hope an anchor in your life? What is your basis for you having hope? Write it down in the space below.

Why Hope is Important to Me

___

CONCLUSION

The fact that you've worked through the entire year improving yourself and your relationship with God is in itself an outstanding achievement in your life. Remember, this study does not end here. As believers, we must continue to work on ourselves and strengthen our walk with God so that we can fulfil our purpose according to his Will. The more you stay the course and develop a more intimate relationship with God, the more life will make sense to you. This is not to say that you will not experience conflict and struggle in life because we all do. However, your life will not succumb to temporary situations. Instead, you will learn from your struggles and see life through a whole new lens.

Your life was meant for so much more than entering a mindless routine leading to a constant barrage of questions that you cannot answer. You were not meant to have an empty feeling of insignificance. You were meant to achieve great things and there is no time like the present to get into gear and OWN your greatness. God is always waiting for you to take that big step and commit yourself to His guidance. You will grow stronger in your ability to *Discern* and attain a level of existence that will bring you a sense of peace and a walk of purpose. Your ability to *Discern* will assist you in many ways and you will utilize this ability as you continue to grow with God. Your time is now. This year of study is your springboard to success, not only for this year, but in the years to come. *Discernment* in life is key. It is time for you to work on your skills so that you can *Discern* more and discover your true purpose in life. This year is only the beginning. Your transformation will have extraordinary lasting effects today, tomorrow and beyond. Your ability to *Discern* will sustain you always.

www.ingramcontent.com/pod-product-compliance
Lightning Source LLC
Chambersburg PA
CBHW031118080526
44587CB00011B/1024